Setting Rules and Limits

HAZELDEN

This workbook is designed to be used with the *Setting Rules and Limits* pamphlet in the *Real Life Parenting Skills Program*. The exercises in this workbook will help you better understand some of the ideas in the pamphlet. The topics and headings in the pamphlet are also in the workbook. Workbook exercises will help you think about how each topic specifically applies to you and your children.

The exercises in this workbook will help you understand three key ideas that will help you set limits for your children:

1. What limits are, why they are important, and how to set them.
2. What consequences are, both natural and structured, and how to set and follow through with structured consequences.
3. How to be a good role model for your children by setting your own personal limits.

WHY AND HOW TO SET LIMITS

✍ Exercise 1: What are limits?

Read each of the following stories. Decide what the problem is and write what you think would be an appropriate limit.

1. *Kareem is twelve years old. He spends much of his free time watching TV or playing video games. His teacher has reported that Kareem is not turning in homework assignments and isn't receiving good grades. In fact, his teacher called for a conference with Kareem's parents and said that Kareem might not pass unless his work improves.*

   What is the problem? _____

   _____

   Describe an appropriate limit: _____

   _____

2. *Elena is a fifteen-year-old who talks on the phone constantly. She receives many phone calls and often talks all evening with her friends. Others in the family are getting fed up because they can't use the phone to call out and their own friends can't call in. The family can't afford to install another phone line.*

What is the problem? _____

_____

Describe an appropriate limit: _____

_____

3. *Rositta is an eight-year-old who loves to ride her bike. She often rides further than she intends to, leaves the apartment complex without telling anyone, and is gone for more than an hour at a time.*

What is the problem? _____

_____

Describe an appropriate limit: _____

_____

✍ *Exercise 2: Why should you set limits for your children?*

Setting rules and limits for children can help them feel more secure, let them know you care about them, and define how you expect them to behave. There are many reasons to set limits, and setting limits can help children in many ways. Determine why limits might be important for your children by answering the questions below.

1. *What limits have you set for your children that are still in effect? Name some below.*

_____

_____

_____

2. *What limits are lacking? What limits do you need to establish?*

Child's name	Limit

3. *Why are limits important for your children? How do you think limits help them?*

_____

_____

_____

✍ *Exercise 3: How to set limits—family meetings.*

Family meetings are one way you can set limits. Family meetings are a good choice when limits need to be set for all the children and when discussing household problems, solutions, and consequences would best be done with all children present.

1. *List problems affecting your household that may best be solved through a family meeting. An example is keeping the house clean.*

a. _____

b. _____

c. _____

d. _____

2. *For each of the problems you identified above, write a limit or rule that you think would help resolve the difficulty.*

Problem	Limit/Rule
a. _____	_____
b. _____	_____
c. _____	_____
d. _____	_____

3. *What steps will you follow to have a family meeting?*

Step one: _____

Step two: _____

Step three: _____

Step four: _____

✍ *Exercise 4: How to set limits—contracts.*

Contracts are another way you can set limits. Contracts work best on a one-on-one basis, just between you and the child whose behavior you wish to change.

1. *For each child, list specific situations you think can be resolved through a contract.*

Child	Problem
_____	_____
_____	_____
_____	_____
_____	_____

2. *For each problem described above, describe a limit you think is appropriate to resolve the situation.*

   a. _____

   b. _____

   c. _____

   d. _____

3. *What steps will you take to make a contract with your child?*

   Step one: _____

   Step two: _____

   Step three: _____

   Step four: _____

4. *When defining a problem, it's important to be very specific. Read each of the stories below and briefly describe the specific problem.*

   a. Lucia is angry with her mother because her mother spent every evening last month away in a treatment program. During that time, Lucia had to stay with an aunt whom she did not like. She also had to attend a different school, so she didn't see her friends at all during that time. Now her mother has finished treatment and is trying to set up a lot of rules. Lucia refuses to do anything her mother asks.

   Describe the specific problem: _____

   _____

   b. Ben is six. He loves to play with his cars and spreads them out all over the apartment. Cars on windowsills, cars on the floor, cars parked beneath tables, cars everywhere. Ben won't pick up any of the cars, even when people have slipped on them or when the house is getting a cleaning for visitors. He says picking them up will ruin his game.

   Describe the specific problem: _____

   _____

5. *For each of the problems described above, name a realistic limit that might resolve the difficulty.*

    a. Lucia: _____

    b. Ben: _____

HOW AND WHEN TO FOLLOW THROUGH WITH CONSEQUENCES

✍ *Exercise 5: Natural consequences.*

1. *Read each of the following stories. Then write what you think might be the natural consequences of the child's action.*

    a. Marissa, a twelve-year-old, refuses to wear a hat of any kind during cold weather. "It's not cool," she says. Marissa has to walk several blocks home from the bus stop. The temperature for the next few days is predicted to be just above zero.

Natural consequence: _____

Natural consequence: _____

    b. Jason is a fourteen-year-old who refuses to change clothes each day. He wears the same few shirts and jeans over and over. Even if it's in the laundry pile, he'll pull out a dirty shirt and wear it. The class picture day is coming up. His mom would like to get a nice photo of Jason to send to family members. Jason says he won't dress up for picture day.

Natural consequence: _____

Natural consequence: _____

    c. Pedro is sixteen. His track coach told him to run every day over summer vacation to keep in shape for the track team tryouts. The track coach likes Pedro and wants to help him succeed in making the track team. Pedro puts off running during the first part of the summer, saying he'll get back into the routine the month before school starts. When August rolls around, he continues to make excuses to avoid a daily running routine.

Natural consequence: _____

Natural consequence: _____

d. *Andy is eight. He wants a special computer game that costs over $50. His parents have told him that if he reads ten books over a two-month period, they'll give him half the money he needs toward the software. And, they'll pay him to do certain household chores until he earns the rest of the money he needs. Andy puts off reading the books and doesn't do many chores. When two months are up, he's read six books and performed just a few of the odd jobs his parents suggested.*

Natural consequence: _____

Natural consequence: _____

2. *Read the following stories and name those situations in which you* ***don't*** *need to step in to enforce consequences.*

a. *Sam is seven. He wants to roller skate but won't wear knee pads or wrist guards. He also refuses to wear a helmet. You warn him that the top three injuries to roller skaters are to head, wrists, and knees.*

What are the likely natural consequences? _____

_____

Let natural consequences take over? _____

Why or why not? _____

_____

b. Anna is sixteen. She just passed her driver's test, so she can drive alone. She wants to drive several of her friends to a school basketball game. The school where the game is being played is twenty miles across the city and in an area that is not familiar to Anna.

What are the likely natural consequences? _____

_____

Let natural consequences take over? _____

Why or why not? _____

_____

c. Brian is thirteen. He wants to go with five of his friends to see a movie at the mall. Several incidents of violence and gang-related fights have been reported at the mall recently. Brian says he'll stick with the group and they'll call for a ride home after they've seen the movie and had something to eat.

What are the likely natural consequences? _____

_____

Let natural consequences take over? _____

Why or why not? _____

_____

3. *Can you name situations with your children when you* **don't** *need to step in to enforce a consequence? What natural consequences will occur?*

   a. _____

   b. _____

   c. _____

✍ *Exercise 6: Structured consequences.*

1. *Read the following stories and write the consequences you would set up to remedy the problem.*

   a. *Janice's room is such a mess that you can't push her door all the way open. She eats snacks and leaves plates and glasses in her room. She drops dirty clothes on the floor, forgetting to put them in the laundry. She leaves doors and drawers open. She often cannot find her schoolbooks or homework.*

Set consequences for Janice
I would like you to _____
because _____
If you don't do _____
then _____

   b. *Darryl is sixteen. Often he leaves the apartment after school without telling anyone where he's going or when he'll be home. You can't rely on him to take care of younger brothers and sisters after school before you get home from work, because you're never sure what his plans are. You also never know if he'll be home to eat supper with the family.*

Set consequences for Darryl
I would like you to _____
because _____
If you don't do _____
then _____

SETTING YOUR OWN LIMITS

🖎 *Exercise 7: Taming the voice of guilt.*

1. *Identify some situations your children might use to make you feel vulnerable to guilt so you will agree to their demands.*

   a. _____

   b. _____

   c. _____

   d. _____

2. *Describe how you will handle each situation listed above.*

   a. _____

   b. _____

   c. _____

   d. _____

🖎 *Exercise 8: My personal limits and consequences.*

1. *List the basic things you need to remain clean and sober over the next three to six months.*

   ### (Examples)

   Exercise three times per week; attend one support group meeting per week; meet with sponsor each week; attend job training each day from 8 A.M. to noon.

Needs
a. _____
b. _____
c. _____
d. _____

2. *For each need listed above, name at least one step you will take to meet that need.*

Actions
a. _____
b. _____
c. _____
d. _____

3. *Suggestion: Call a family meeting and share this exercise with your children. Show them your needs list and your actions list. Tell them these are limits you've set for yourself for the next three to six months. Then, ask them to help you set consequences for yourself if you don't meet these goals. Your kids will enjoy turning the tables on you!*

Action	Consequence
a. _____	_____
	_____
b. _____	_____
	_____
c. _____	_____
	_____
d. _____	_____
	_____

✍ *Exercise 9: Action steps.*

After finishing the exercises in this workbook, describe some goals you've set for yourself in each of the areas we covered.

1. *How to set limits.*

(Example)

I will set up a family meeting to clarify my expectations about getting household chores done.

a. _____

_____

b. _____

_____

c. _____

_____

2. *How to set consequences.*

(Example)

I will discuss a problem behavior with my children and ask them to help choose the consequence.

a. _____

_____

b. _____

_____

c. _____

_____

3. Setting my own limits.

(Example)

I will attend at least one support group meeting each week. I will discuss with my children why I need to attend the meeting and how that helps me maintain my recovery, an important priority.

a. _____

_____

b. _____

_____

c. _____

_____

Rock Guitar Playing
Grade Two

Compiled by
Tony Skinner and Merv Young
on behalf of
Registry Of Guitar Tutors
www.RGT.org

Printed and bound in Great Britain

A CIP record for this publication is available from the British Library
ISBN: 978-1-905908-32-5

Published by Registry Publications

Registry Mews, Wilton Rd, Bexhill, Sussex, TN40 1HY

Cover photo by Andreas Gradin/Fotolia. Design by JAK Images.

Compiled by

v.20111111

Contents

Page

Introduction

This book is part of a progressive series of ten handbooks designed for rock guitarists who wish to develop their playing and obtain a qualification. Although the primary intention of these handbooks is to prepare candidates for the Registry Of Guitar Tutors (RGT) rock guitar exams, the series provides a comprehensive structure that will help develop the abilities of any guitarist interested in rock music, whether or not intending to take an exam.

Those preparing for an exam should use this handbook in conjunction with the *Syllabus for Rock Guitar Playing* and the *Rock Guitar Exam Information Booklet* – both freely downloadable from the RGT website: **www.RGT.org**

Exam Outline

There are three components to this exam, each of which is briefly outlined below:

❶   **Prepared Performances.** The performance, along to backing tracks, of special arrangements of two classic rock pieces.

❷   **Improvisation.** This is in two parts: firstly, improvisation of a lead guitar solo over a previously unseen chord progression, followed by improvisation of a rhythm guitar part over the same chord progression. Playing will be to a backing track provided by the examiner.

❸   **Aural Assessment.** This will consist of a 'Rhythm Test' (repeating the rhythm of a riff), a 'Pitch Test' (accurately reproducing a riff on the guitar) and a 'Chord Recognition Test' (recognising chord types).

Mark Scheme

The maximum marks available for each component are:

- Prepared Performances: 60 marks (30 marks per piece).
- Improvisation: 30 marks.
- Aural Assessment: 10 marks.

To pass the exam candidates need a total of 65 marks. Candidates achieving 75 marks will be awarded a Merit certificate, or a Distinction certificate for 85 marks or above.

Tuning

For exam purposes guitars should be tuned to Standard Concert Pitch (A=440Hz). The use of an electronic tuner or other tuning aid is permitted. The examiner will not assist with tuning other than to, upon request, offer an E or A note to tune to.

Notation

Within this handbook, scales and chords are illustrated in three formats: traditional notation, tablature and fretboxes – thereby ensuring that there is no doubt as to how to play each scale or chord. Each of these methods of notation is explained below.

<u>Traditional Notation:</u>   Each line, and space between lines, represents a different note. Leger lines are used to extend the stave for low or high notes. For scales, fret and string numbers are printed below the notation: fret-hand fingering is shown with the numbers 1 2 3 4, with 0 indicating an open string; string numbers are shown in a circle. The example below shows a two-octave A natural minor scale.

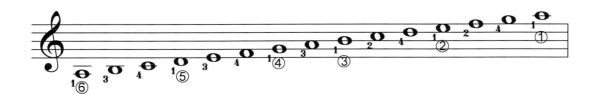

<u>Tablature:</u>   Horizontal lines represent the strings (with the top line being the high E string). The numbers on the string lines refer to the frets. 0 on a line means play that string open (unfretted). The example below means play at the second fret on the third string.

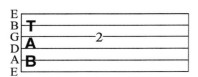

<u>Fretboxes:</u>   Vertical lines represent the strings – with the line furthest to the right representing the high E string. Horizontal lines represent the frets. The numbers on the lines show the recommended fingering. 1 represents the index finger, 2 = the long middle finger, 3 = the ring finger, 4 = the little finger. The example below means play with the second finger at the second fret on the G string.

E A D G B E

5

Fingering Options

The fret-hand fingerings that have been chosen are those that are most likely to be effective for the widest range of players at this level. However, there are a variety of alternative fingerings that could be used, and any systematic and effective fingerings that produce a good musical result will be acceptable; there is no requirement to use the exact fingerings shown within this handbook.

Exam Entry

An exam entry form is provided at the rear of this handbook. This is the only valid entry form for the RGT rock guitar playing exams.

Please note that if the entry form is detached and lost, it will not be replaced under any circumstances and the candidate will be required to obtain a replacement handbook to obtain another entry form.

The entry form includes a unique entry code to enable online entry via the RGT website **www.RGT.org**

About Registry of Guitar Tutors (RGT)

- RGT was established in 1992 and is the world's largest organisation of guitar educators.

- RGT organises exams in a wide range of guitar styles, from beginner to professional Diploma level, in numerous countries around the world.

- RGT exams are operated in partnership with London College of Music Exams, which was founded in 1887 and is one of the world's most respected music examination boards.

- The qualifications are awarded and certificated by the University of West London and, from Grade One onwards, are accredited by Ofqual and have been placed on the Qualifications and Credit Framework. From Grade Six onwards, RGT exams attract UCAS points which can be used towards university entrance.

For more information about RGT visit www.RGT.org

Prepared Performances

Candidates should choose and perform TWO of the following classic rock pieces:

❶ Day Tripper – The Beatles

❷ Wonderful Tonight – Eric Clapton

❸ Should I Stay Or Should I Go – The Clash

Obtaining the notation and audio

These pieces have been specifically arranged for the RGT Grade Two Rock Guitar Playing exam and are notated in TAB and standard notation in the publication *Graded Guitar Songs – 9 Rock Classics for Beginning Level Guitarists**. This also includes a CD that features each track being performed in full, as well as a backing track for each piece for the candidate to perform with during the exam. These tracks have been specially recorded to suit RGT exam requirements.

*For copyright ownership reasons, the notation and audio tracks for these pieces cannot be included in this RGT grade handbook. However, they are all included in the book *Graded Guitar Songs – 9 Rock Classics for Beginning Level Guitarists*, which is available from *www.BooksForGuitar.com* or can be ordered from most music stores. *Graded Guitar Songs – 9 Rock Classics for Beginning Level Guitarists* contains all performance pieces that are required for the RGT rock guitar playing exams Grades One, Two and Three.

Exam format

Candidates' performances should be accurate reproductions of the specially arranged versions of the pieces as notated and recorded in the book *Graded Guitar Songs – 9 Rock Classics for Beginning Level Guitarists*. Alternative fingerings and playing positions to those shown in the book can be adopted if preferred, provided the overall musical result is not altered from the recorded version.

Performances do not need to be from memory; candidates should remember to bring their book to the exam should they wish to refer to the notation.

The performances should be played along to the specially recorded backing tracks supplied on the CD that is included with the book *Graded Guitar Songs – 9 Rock Classics for Beginning Level Guitarists*. Alternative recordings of the pieces will not be accepted as backing tracks. There is no need to bring your CD to the exam, as the examiner will provide the necessary backing tracks during the exam.

Prior to the performance commencing, candidates will be allowed a brief 'soundcheck' so that they can choose their sound and volume level. Candidates can use either a clean or a distorted guitar sound for their performance of these tracks, and can bring their own distortion or other effects units to the exam *providing that* they can set them up promptly and unaided.

In order to achieve a high mark in this section of the exam, performances should be fully accurate and very confidently presented. Timing, clarity and technical control should be totally secure throughout, and some expressive qualities (such as varying the dynamics of the performance) should be displayed.

Performance Tips

Day Tripper – The Beatles

The RGT arrangement of this piece is in the original key of E major. The intro riff moves smoothly across the three bass strings.

The intro riff repeats five times before the verse starts, so count the repeats carefully and listen for the lead guitar playing the vocal melody as the cue for the beginning of the verse.

The move from the last note of the verse in bar 10 to the first F#5 power chord in the chorus is tricky to execute smoothly so practice this transition carefully. There are two different rhythm patterns used on the chords in the chorus, so follow the notation carefully and listen to the recorded track to ensure you are familiar with how these are to be played.

The riff that occurs in the bridge (i.e. bars 23 to 24) may require practice to perform smoothly – as, to avoid a wide finger stretch, a shift of fingerboard position may be required to reach all the notes – so you'll need to take care to adopt a fingering approach that enables fluency and accuracy.

Although not indicated in the notation, there are instances where the use of a hammer-on may produce a smoother, more fluent sound and this technique can be utilised if preferred. In bar 1 the G# note on fret 4 can be produced by hammering-on from the preceding G note on fret 3. Similarly the E note on fret 2 at the end of bar 2 can be played using a hammer-on from the open D string that precedes it. If using a hammer-on, bring the appropriate fretting-hand finger down firmly onto the note to ensure that it sounds clearly and make sure that the rhythm of the notes is not altered by employing this technique.

Wonderful Tonight – Eric Clapton

The RGT arrangement of this piece is in the original key of G major. There are several different guitar parts on the original artist's version of this track; the RGT arrangement combines elements of several of these parts – so follow the notation carefully throughout to ensure that your performance is accurate to the RGT arrangement.

The slow tempo and ballad feel of this tune means the pitch accuracy of the string bends in the intro section is particularly important. Similarly, the slide and hammer-on in bar 8 both need to be executed smoothly and cleanly as demonstrated on the recording.

In the opening bar of the verse (bar 9) the high D note at fret 10 should be held down and allowed to ring out for a count of 3 beats. Whilst this note is ringing the open string pattern on the D, G and B strings can be picked. (Note that, if preferred, this 'optional' open string pattern in bar 9 can be omitted from the exam performance to ensure a smooth transition to the D chord in bar 10.)

Care is needed for the chord changes that occur throughout the remainder of the verse, chorus and bridge sections to ensure they are executed smoothly and cleanly. Practise the chords carefully to maintain an even rhythm pattern, using whichever picking method feels most effective, e.g. a plectrum only or plectrum and fingers.

This arrangement features a number of techniques such as string bends and slides. Practise each of the string bends on its own to ensure the string is being bent up to the correct pitch. Using at least 2 fingers to execute a string bend will give greater control and accuracy. Also, make sure the starting note of each bend doesn't ring out for too long and that this note rings out clearly when bending back down to it. For the slide that occurs in bar 8, move the fretting-hand finger smoothly and confidently from fret 12 to 13; the note on fret 12 has no real rhythmic value so don't let it ring out for too long.

Should I Stay Or Should I Go – The Clash

The RGT arrangement of this piece is in the original key of D major. The 'percussive' strums in bar 2 are performed by resting the fingers of the fretting hand gently against the strings to mute them whilst strumming. Count the rhythm carefully in bar 4 to ensure the hammer-on is played correctly – i.e. at the start of the third beat of the bar.

The open string 'vamps' that occur between a number of the chord changes throughout the piece help to maintain the energy and fluency of the music. However, the chord changes still need to be executed smoothly and fluently, especially the tricky move from the G chord to the F chord that occurs in bar 11. Practise all of these chord changes carefully to ensure that the rhythm remains accurate and consistent even when playing the open strings between the chords. Try to keep your strumming hand moving evenly and smoothly all the time when practicing these chord changes – this will help you learn how quickly your fretting hand has to move to ensure the changes are accurate and rhythmically secure.

Follow the notation and listen to the track carefully in the chorus to ensure you are familiar with the rhythm patterns that are required there. The chords need to change smoothly and the rhythm is quite tricky to execute at first. In particular the move from the G chord to the F chord and back to the G chord in bars 21 and 22 will require some careful practice to execute smoothly.

The track features a number of rests (i.e. silences) between chords; look out for these when playing and ensure you silence the strings when a rest is notated.

Improvisation

The candidate will be shown a previously unseen chord chart in $^4_4$ time. This will consist of an 8-bar chord progression, which will be played five times non-stop (via a pre-recorded backing track).

- During the first verse, the candidate should just listen to the track while reading the chord chart.

- A 4-beat count-in will be given and then during the next two verses, the candidate should improvise a lead guitar solo.

- A 4-beat count-in will be given and then during the last two verses, the candidate should improvise a rhythm guitar part.

- The backing track will end with the first chord of the progression played once.

Candidates will be given a short time to study the chord chart and will then be allowed a brief 'soundcheck' with the track prior to the performance commencing, so that they can choose their sound and volume level. Candidates can bring their own distortion or other effects units to the exam *providing that* they can set them up promptly and unaided.

The backing track will include drums, bass and rhythm guitar for the first three verses, but in the last two verses the recorded rhythm guitar part will be omitted so that the candidate can perform their own rhythm guitar part.

The rhythm guitar part that is recorded on the backing track gives an indication of the standard of rhythm playing that is expected for this section of the exam. Candidates do not need to reproduce exactly the rhythm part that is recorded on the backing track. They should, however, strive to perform a rhythm part that is stylistically appropriate and with a "feel" that is in keeping with the backing track. Part of the assessment here will be centred on the candidate's ability to listen and then perform an appropriate rhythm part.

The range of chords that may appear in the backing tracks for this grade is detailed on following pages. As the chord progression will be previously unseen by the candidate, the candidate will need to be fully familiar with all the chords listed for the grade in order to be properly prepared for the chord progressions that will occur in the exam. Each chord progression will consist of chords grouped together into appropriate keys. Several examples of the type of chord progression that will occur at this grade are provided at the end of this chapter.

In order to improvise a lead guitar solo accurately and effectively, candidates will need to learn a range of appropriate scales upon which to base their improvisation. The first chord in the progression will be the key chord and will, therefore, indicate the scale that would generally be best to use for improvising a lead solo; the recommended scales that could be used to improvise over the chord progressions at this grade are provided later in this chapter. Although other scale options and improvisation approaches exist, it is highly recommended that candidates acquire a thorough knowledge of the scales listed for the grade, as these will provide a core foundation for improvisation at the appropriate level of technical development. However, providing they produce an effective musical result, other appropriate scale choices or improvisation approaches will also be acceptable.

The examiner will not provide any advice regarding identifying the key or guidance on which scale to use.

↓ Volume Changes

When playing your lead guitar improvisation, your volume will need to be loud enough to be clearly heard over the accompaniment. When switching to rhythm playing, during the improvisation section of the exam, you will almost certainly need to quickly adjust the volume of your guitar, as the settings you have used for single-note lead playing may be too loud and could overpower the accompaniment if used when strumming chords during the rhythm playing.

There are various ways this volume change could be made, but at this grade the most straightforward method would be one of the following:

• Turn down the volume control on your guitar.

• Use the pick-up selector on your guitar to switch to a pick-up with a lower output, or (if your guitar has more than one volume control) to a pick-up that you have pre-adjusted to a lower volume setting.

• If you are using your own distortion/overdrive unit for lead playing, turn this off and use a quieter clean sound for rhythm playing.

Prior to the exam, it is important to practise and become adept at making this volume change – as during the exam it will need to be done quickly and smoothly during the last bar of the lead guitar section, so that you are ready to begin the rhythm playing section in time.

Chords

Here is the range of chords that may occur in the chord progressions for this grade.

•	Major chords:	A, C, D, E, F*, G
•	Minor chords:	Am, Dm, Em, F#m*
•	Dominant 7th chords:	A7, D7, E7

Open position chords are expected at this grade, except for the partial-barré chords marked * above.

A major

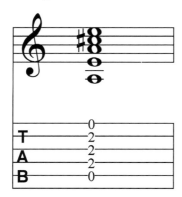 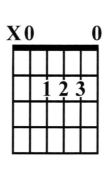

C major

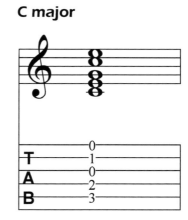 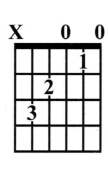

D major

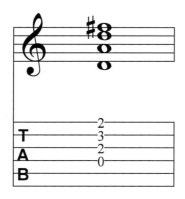 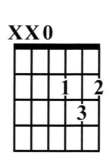

E major

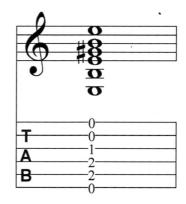 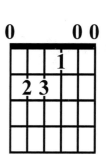

F major

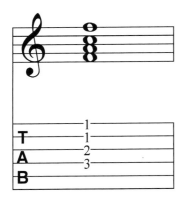
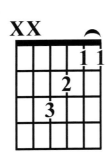

G major

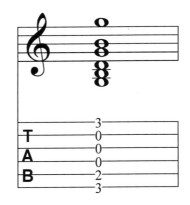
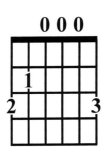

A minor

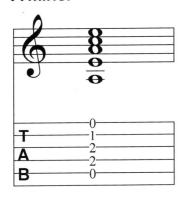

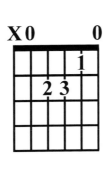

D minor

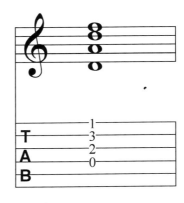
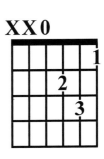

E minor

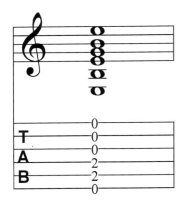
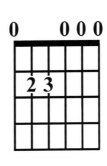

F# minor

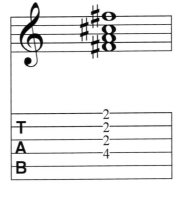
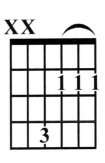

A Dominant 7

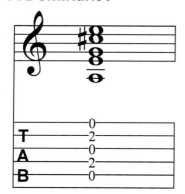 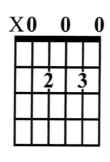

D Dominant 7

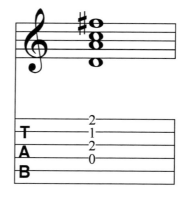 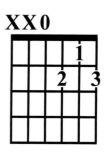

E Dominant 7

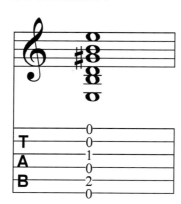 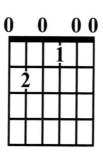

Scales

Here is the range of scales recommended for use during the lead guitar improvisation section of the exam at this grade.

Scale:	Range of chords that may be included in the exam progression:
A pentatonic major: A blues: A natural minor:	A D E F#m A7 D7 E7 C G Am C Dm Em F G

Improvisation using two-octave fretted scales is expected at this grade.

A pentatonic major scale – 2 octaves
A B C# E F# A

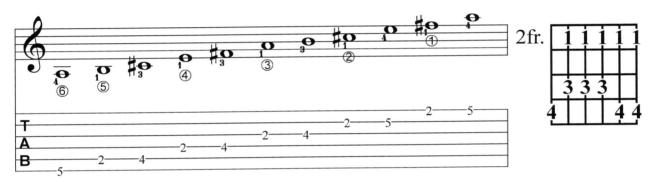

A blues scale – 2 octaves
A C D Eb E G A

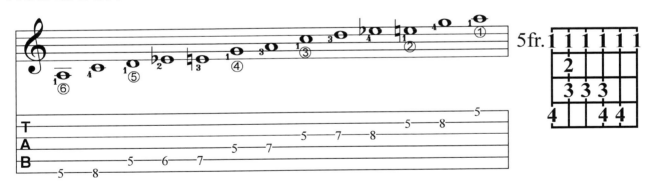

A natural minor scale – 2 octaves
A B C D E F G A

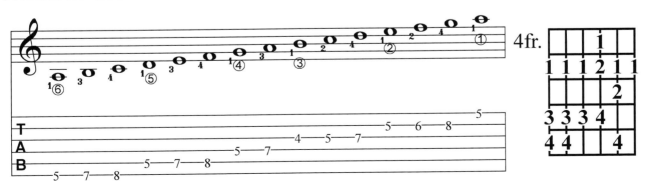

Performance Advice

In order to attain maximum marks in this section of the exam, the performance needs to be fully accurate and confident in execution, with a high level of clarity and fluency appropriate to the grade. There should be some evidence of stylistic interpretation, inventiveness and creativity.

As the improvised rhythm playing will be performed over a recorded backing track, the emphasis will be on developing key performance skills such as rhythmic security and fluency. Dynamic markings are not included on the chord charts, to enable candidates to focus on their own rhythmic and dynamic interpretation.

The improvised lead solo should be accurate in terms of note selection and timing in relation to the accompaniment. There should be some evidence of melodic phrasing and shaping. Specialist techniques such as string bends, slides and slurs can be attempted by candidates if they wish, but a high level of skill in using these techniques is not expected at this grade.

Performance Tips

➢ Try to use the short period of study time, when you're first shown the chord chart, as effectively as possible by looking through the chart to ensure you are confident with the chords that occur and with your choice of scale.

➢ During the first verse of the backing track, follow the chord chart carefully and get ready to start your lead guitar improvisation after the 4 beat count-in.

➢ Listen carefully to the backing track throughout the performance to ensure that your lead and rhythm playing is rhythmically secure; try to make your playing relate to what the bass and drums are playing.

➢ Keep an awareness of where you are in the chord chart, so that the 4 beat count-in to commence your rhythm playing doesn't take you by surprise – as the examiner will not re-start the backing track once it is underway.

➢ During the lead improvising listen carefully to what you are playing to make it sound as musically effective as you can, and try playing the notes in musical phrases to enhance the impact of what you play.

➢ Prior to exam day, when preparing for this section of the exam ensure that you are completely confident knowing, and changing between, all the chords that may occur; during the exam itself you can then focus on playing the chords as confidently and musically as possible.

➢ The example chord charts that are provided overleaf give an indication of what to expect in the exam, but these are not the actual charts that will be given. In preparing for this section of the exam you are advised to download all these example backing tracks to ensure you are comfortable with improvising both lead and rhythm parts over the range of tempos and styles indicated by these examples.

Example Chord Progressions

The following are examples of the type of chord progression candidates may be presented with in this section of the exam. Please note that the scale suggestions shown above each progression will NOT appear in the charts presented during the exam.

Improvisation Chart Example 1

A pentatonic major scale could be used to improvise over this progression.

$\frac{4}{4}$ A		A		E		E	
F♯m		F♯m		D		E	‖

Improvisation Chart Example 2

A pentatonic major scale could be used to improvise over this progression.

$\frac{4}{4}$ A		A		F♯m		F♯m	
D		D		A		E	‖

Improvisation Chart Example 3

A blues scale could be used to improvise over this progression.

| $\frac{4}{4}$ A7 | A7 | D7 | D7 | |

| E7 | E7 | G | E7 | ‖

Improvisation Chart Example 4

A blues scale could be used to improvise over this progression.

| $\frac{4}{4}$ A7 | A7 | C | C | |

| D7 | D7 | E7 | G | ‖

Improvisation Chart Example 5

A natural minor scale could be used to improvise over this progression.

| $\frac{4}{4}$ Am | Am | F | F | |

| G | G | Dm | Em | ‖

Improvisation Chart Example 6

A natural minor scale could be used to improvise over this progression.

$\frac{4}{4}$ Am		Am		G		G	
	Dm		Dm		Em		G

It is important to note that the sample chord progressions provided above are supplied purely to provide examples of the *type* of chord progression that may occur in the exam. These examples are NOT the actual chord progressions that candidates will be given in the exam.

Aural Assessment

Candidates' aural abilities will be assessed via a series of three aural tests:
• Rhythm test   • Pitch test   • Chord recognition test.

Rhythm Test

A riff is played three times via a recording. During the third playing the candidate is required to clap along with the exact *rhythm* of the riff.

At this grade, the riff will be two bars in length. The time signature will be $^4_4$. Note durations will be limited to quarter notes (crotchets) and eighth notes (quavers).

Examples of the *type* of riffs that will occur at this grade are shown below, with the rhythm to be clapped notated below the tab.

Pitch Test

The riff from the rhythm test is played two further times with a click track. A gap is left after each playing, so that the candidate can practice the riff. Then, after a one-bar count-in, the candidate is required to play along with a click track, accurately reproducing the riff on the guitar.

At this grade, the range of scales from which the riff will be derived is limited to those listed in the improvisation section of this handbook, i.e. A pentatonic major scale, A blues scale and A natural minor scale. The riff will start on the keynote. The examiner will state which scale the riff is taken from.

Below are some examples of the *type* of riffs that will occur at this grade in the rhythm and pitch tests.

Example 1 (from A blues scale)

Example 2 (from A natural minor scale)

Example 3 (from A natural minor scale)

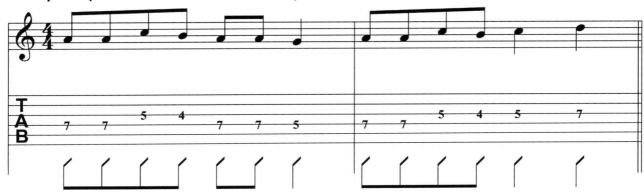

Example 4 (from A pentatonic major scale)

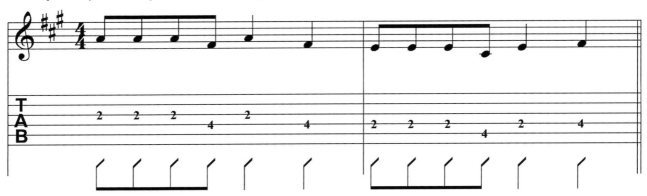

Chord Recognition Test

This test involves recognising chords as either major, minor or dominant seventh: after hearing a short chord progression once, candidates should state whether it contained either all major chords, all minor chords or all dominant seventh chords. Candidates must not use the guitar to aid their answer.

The range of chords used in this test is limited to those listed in the improvisation section of this handbook, i.e. A, C, D, E, F, G, Am, Dm, Em, F#m, A7, D7, E7.

Below are some examples of the *type* of chord progressions that will occur at this grade in the chord recognition tests.

Example 1

| $\frac{4}{4}$ A | D | E | A | ||

major

Example 2

| $\frac{4}{4}$ Am | Dm | Em | Am | ||

minor

Example 3

| $\frac{4}{4}$ A7 | D7 | E7 | A7 | ||

dominant 7

Listen and Practise

Audio recordings of all the above sample tests can be downloaded from
www.DownloadsForGuitar.com

It is important to note that the example tests provided above are supplied purely to provide examples of the *type* of test that may occur in the exam. These examples are NOT necessarily the actual tests that candidates will be given in the exam.

The Specialists in Guitar Education

Registry of Guitar Tutors

Exam Entry Form
Rock Guitar Grade ②

ONLINE ENTRY – AVAILABLE FOR UK CANDIDATES ONLY

For **UK candidates**, entries and payments can be made online at www.RGT.org, using the entry code below. You will be able to pay the entry fee by credit or debit card at a secure payment page on the website.

Your unique and confidential exam entry code is:

RB-5173-AZ

Keep this unique code confidential, as it can only be used once. Once you have entered online, you should sign this form overleaf. **You must bring this signed form to your exam and hand it to the examiner in order to be admitted to the exam room.**

If NOT entering online, please complete BOTH sides of this form and return to the address overleaf.

SESSION (Spring/Summer/Winter): _____ YEAR: _____

Dates/times NOT available: _____

Note: Only name *specific* dates (and times on those dates) when it would be <u>*absolutely impossible*</u> for you to attend due to important prior commitments (such as pre-booked overseas travel) which cannot be cancelled. We will then endeavour to avoid scheduling an exam session in your area on those dates. In fairness to all other candidates in your area, **only list dates on which it would be impossible for you to attend.** An entry form that blocks out unreasonable periods may be returned. (Exams may be held on any day of the week including, but not exclusively, weekends. Exams may be held within or outside of the school term.)

Candidate Details: *Please write as clearly as possible using BLOCK CAPITALS*

Candidate Name (as to appear on certificate): _____

Address: _____

_____ Postcode: _____

Tel. No. (day): _____ (mobile): _____

IMPORTANT: Take care to write your email address below as clearly as possible, as your exam entry acknowledgement and your exam appointment details will be sent to this email address. Only provide an email address that is in regular monitored use.

Email:_____
Where an email address is provided your exam correspondence will be sent by email only, and not by post. This will ensure your exam correspondence will reach you sooner.

Teacher Details *(if applicable)*

Teacher Name (as to appear on certificate): _____

RGT Tutor Code (if applicable):_____

Address: _____

_____ Postcode: _____

Tel. No. (day): _____ (mobile): _____

Email:_____

RGT Rock Guitar Official Entry Form

The standard LCM entry form is NOT valid for RGT exam entries.
Entry to the exam is only possible via this original form.
Photocopies of this form will not be accepted under any circumstances.

- Completion of this entry form is an agreement to comply with the current syllabus requirements and conditions of entry published at www.RGT.org. Where candidates are entered for exams by a teacher, parent or guardian that person hereby takes responsibility that the candidate is entered in accordance with the current syllabus requirements and conditions of entry.

- If you are being taught by an *RGT registered* tutor, please hand this completed form to your tutor and request him/her to administer the entry on your behalf.

- For candidates with special needs, a letter giving details should be attached.

Exam Fee: £_____   Late Entry Fee (if applicable): £_____

Total amount submitted: £_____

Cheques or postal orders should be made payable to Registry of Guitar Tutors.

Details of conditions of entry, entry deadlines and exam fees are obtainable from the RGT website: www.RGT.org

Once an entry has been accepted, entry fees cannot be refunded.

CANDIDATE INFORMATION (UK Candidates only)

In order to meet our obligations in monitoring the implementation of equal opportunities policies, UK candidates are required to supply the information requested below. The information provided will in no way whatsoever influence the marks awarded during the exam.

Date of birth: _____ Age: _____ Gender – please circle: male / female

Ethnicity (please enter 2 digit code from chart below): _____ Signed: _____

ETHNIC ORIGIN CLASSIFICATIONS (If you prefer not to say, write '17' in the space above.)

White: **01 British**   **02 Irish**   **03 Other white background**

Mixed: **04 White & black Caribbean**   **05 White & black African**   **06 White & Asian**   **07 Other mixed background**

Asian or Asian British: **08 Indian**   **09 Pakistani**   **10 Bangladeshi**   **11 Other Asian background**

Black or Black British: **12 Caribbean**   **13 African**   **14 Other black background**

Chinese or Other Ethnic Group: **15 Chinese**   **16 Other**   **17 Prefer not to say**

I understand and accept the current syllabus regulations and conditions of entry for this exam as specified on the RGT website.

Signed by candidate (if aged 18 or over) _____ Date _____

If candidate is under 18, this form should be signed by a parent/guardian/teacher (circle which applies):

Signed _____ Name_____ Date_____

UK ENTRIES

See overleaf for details of how to enter online OR return this form to:
Registry of Guitar Tutors, Registry Mews, 11 to 13 Wilton Road, Bexhill-on-Sea, E. Sussex, TN40 1HY
(If you have submitted your entry online do NOT post this form, instead you need to sign it above and hand it to the examiner on the day of your exam.)
To contact the RGT office telephone 01424 222222 or Email office@RGT.org

NON-UK ENTRIES

To locate the address within your country that entry forms should be sent to, and to view exam fees in your currency, visit the RGT website **www.RGT.org** and navigate to the 'RGT Worldwide' section.